INTERMEDIATE+

Christmas Around the World

12 PIANO ARRANGEMENTS IN PROGRESSIVE ORDER

CONTENTS

FUM, FUM, FUM... 2

LOS PECES EN EL RÍO
(The Fishes in the River)..................................... 4

THE HURON CAROL 6

DORMI, DORMI, BEL BAMBIN
(Sleep, Sleep, Lovely Child) 8

GO TELL IT ON THE MOUNTAIN 11

DORS, MA COLOMBE
(Sleep, Little Dove)... 14

THE WEXFORD CAROL 16

WŚRÓD NOCNEJ CISZY
(In Midnight's Silence) 18

O TANNENBAUM (O Christmas Tree)......... 21

UKRAINIAN BELL CAROL............................... 24

GESÙ BAMBINO (The Infant Jesus)........... 27

CANTIQUE DE NÖEL (O Holy Night).......... 30

ISBN 978-1-70517-015-1

Visit Hal Leonard Online at
www.halleonard.com

World headquarters, contact:
Hal Leonard
7777 West Bluemound Road
Milwaukee, WI 53213
Email: info@halleonard.com

In Europe, contact:
Hal Leonard Europe Limited
1 Red Place
London, W1K 6PL
Email: info@halleonardeurope.com

In Australia, contact:
Hal Leonard Australia Pty. Ltd.
4 Lentara Court
Cheltenham, Victoria, 3192 Australia
Email: info@halleonard.com.au

Fum, Fum, Fum

Traditional Catalonian
Arranged by Jennifer Linn

Animato

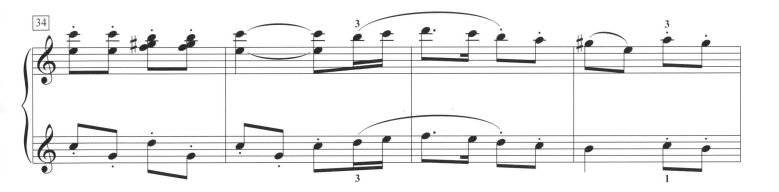

Los Peces en el Río

(The Fishes in the River)

Traditional Latin American
Arranged by Jennifer Linn

Lively

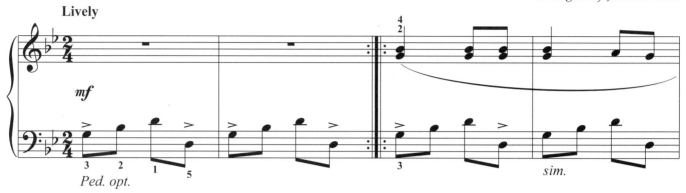

The Huron Carol

Traditional Canadian
Arranged by Jennifer Linn

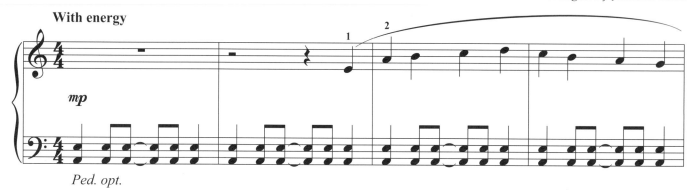

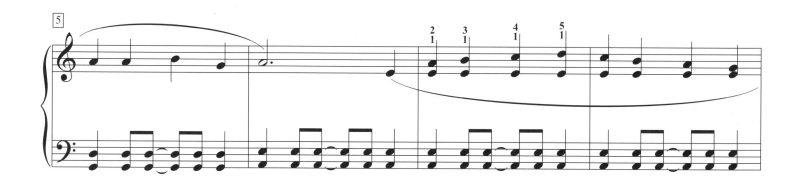

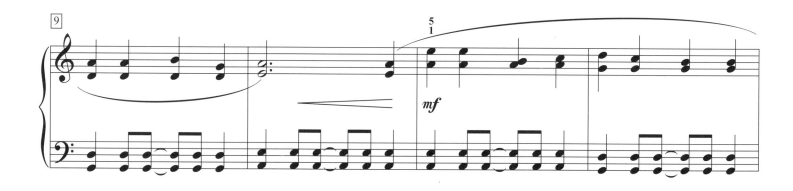

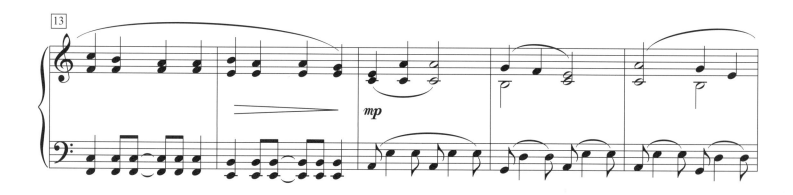

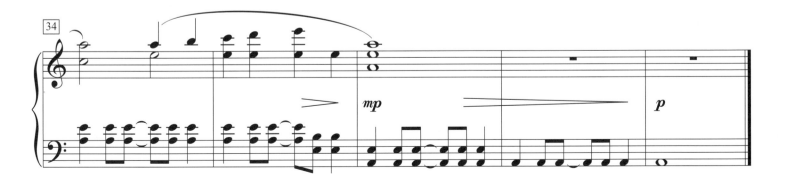

Dormi, Dormi, Bel Bambin
(Sleep, Sleep, Lovely Child)

Traditional Italian
Arranged by Jennifer Linn

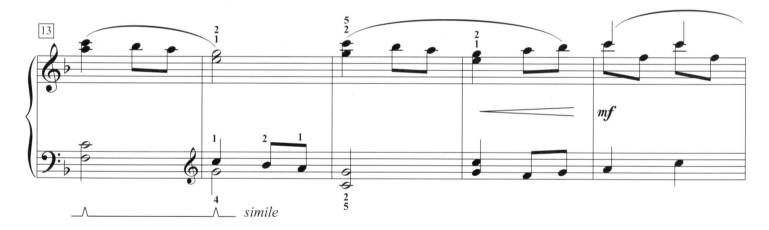

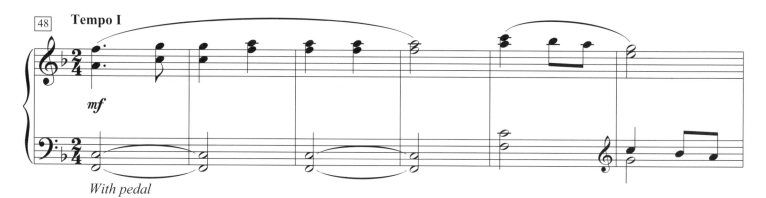

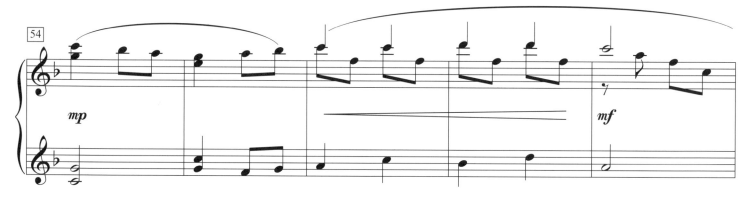

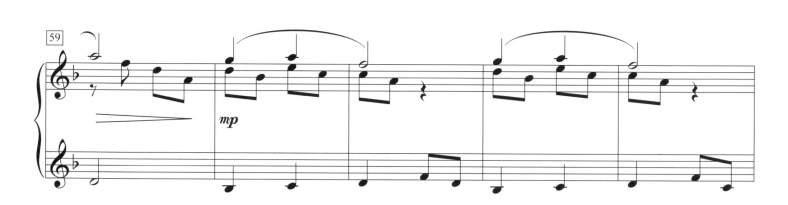

Go Tell It On the Mountain

African-American Spiritual
Arranged by Jennifer Linn

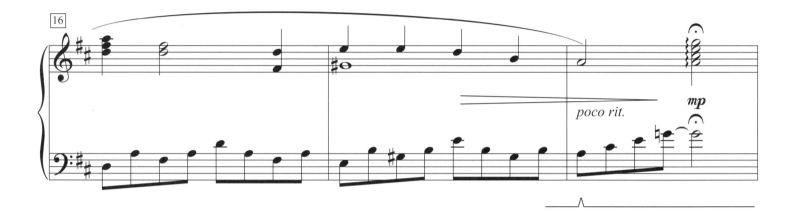

Dors, Ma Colombe
(Sleep, Little Dove)

Traditional Alsatian
Arranged by Jennifer Linn

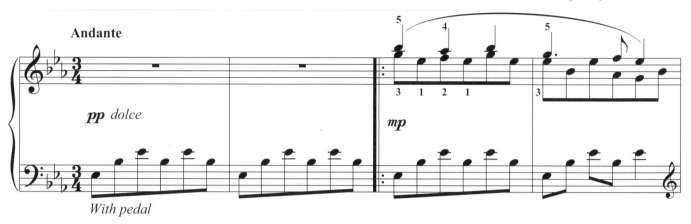

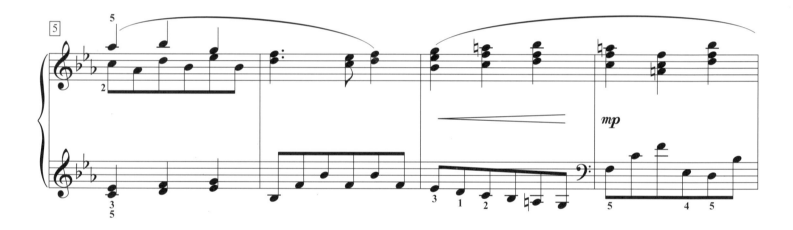

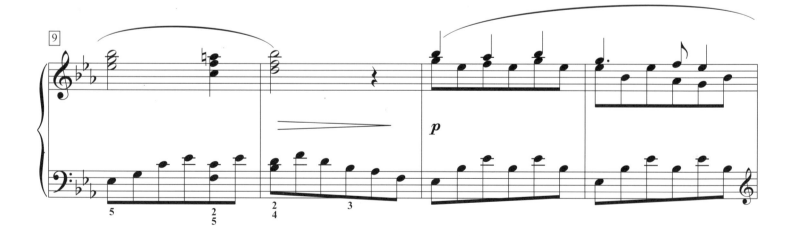

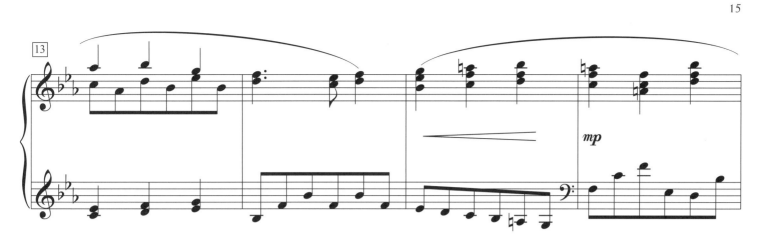

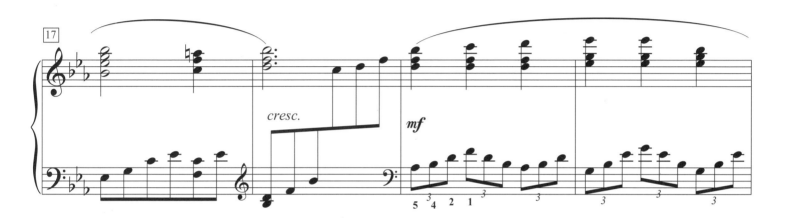

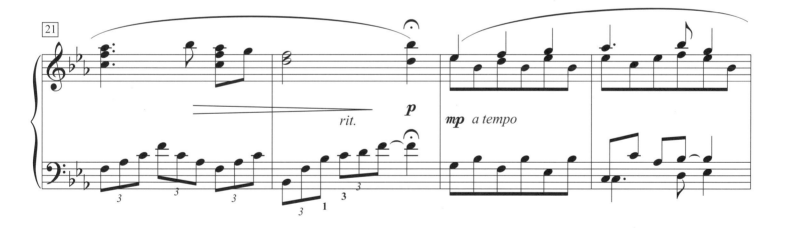

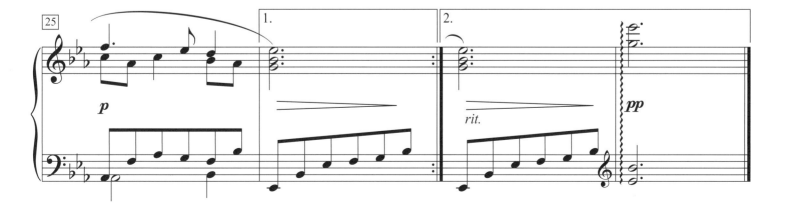

The Wexford Carol

Traditional Irish
Arranged by Jennifer Linn

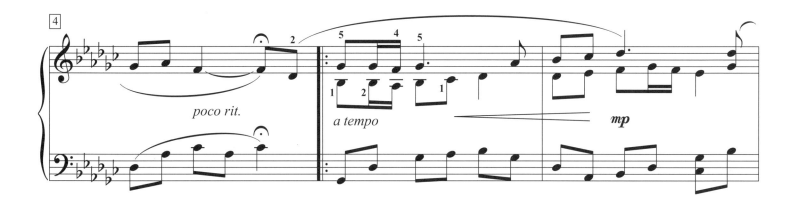

Wśród nocnej ciszy

(In Midnight's Silence)

Traditional Polish
Arranged by Jennifer Linn

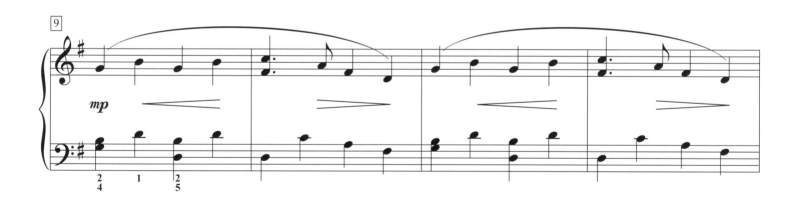

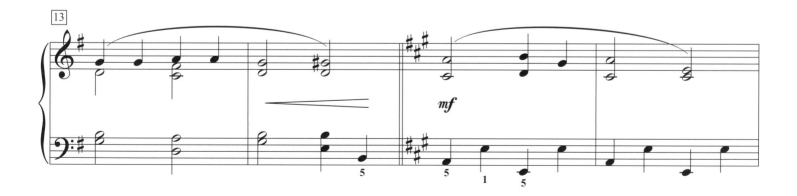

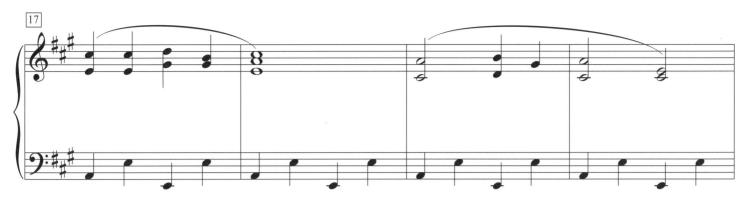

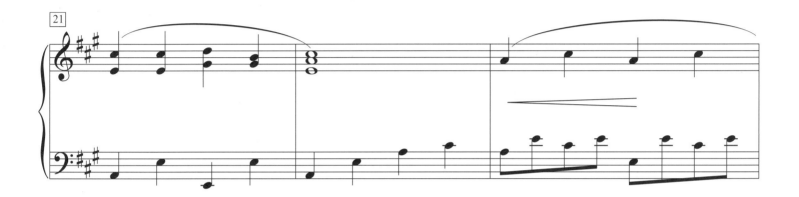

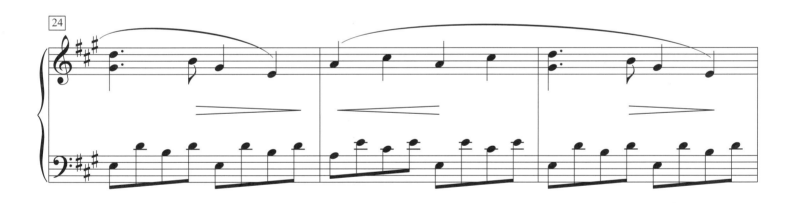

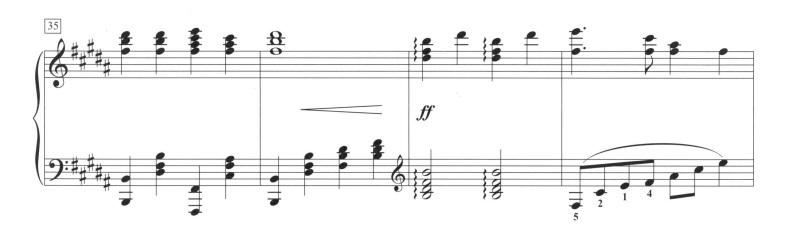

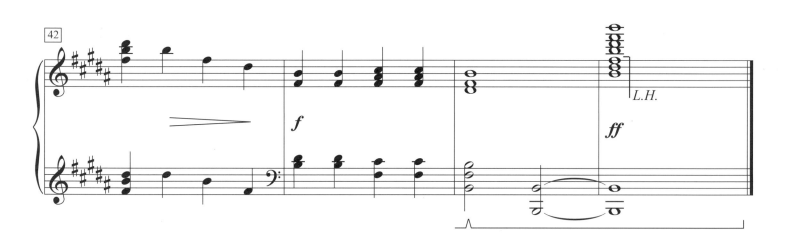

O Tannenbaum
(O Christmas Tree)

Traditional German
Arranged by Jennifer Linn

Peacefully

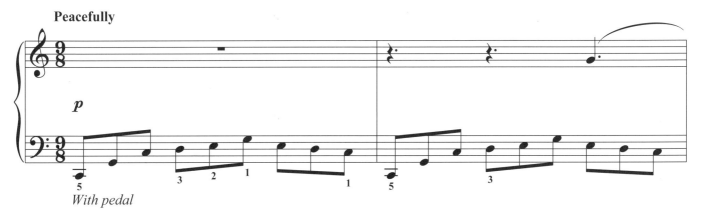

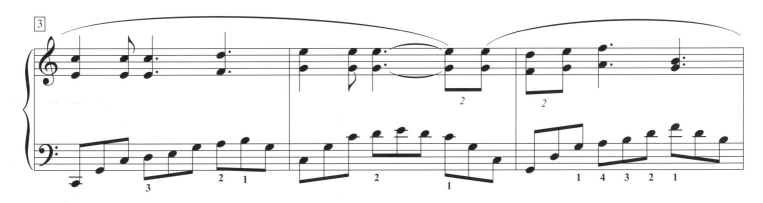

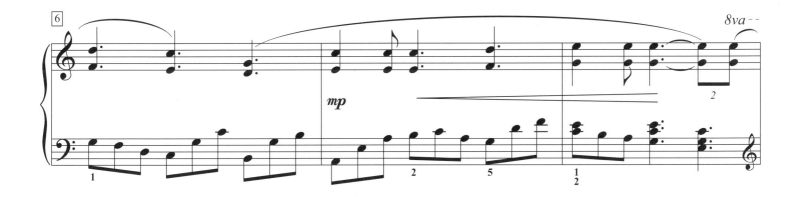

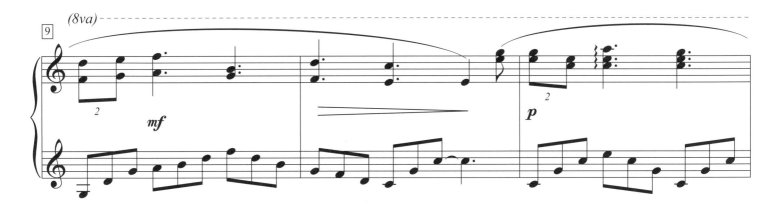

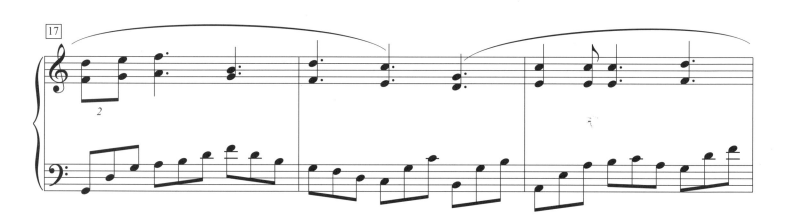

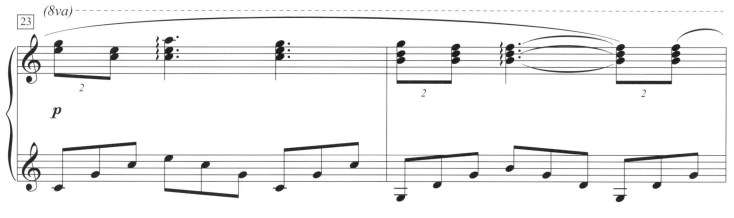

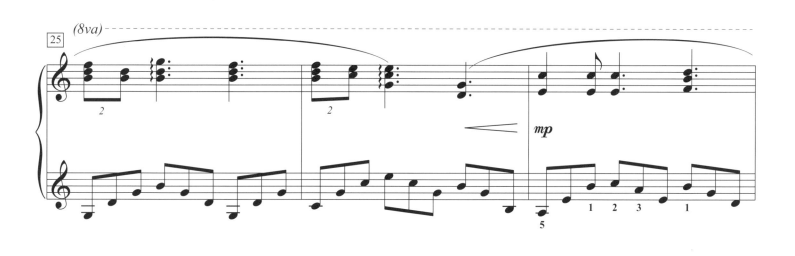

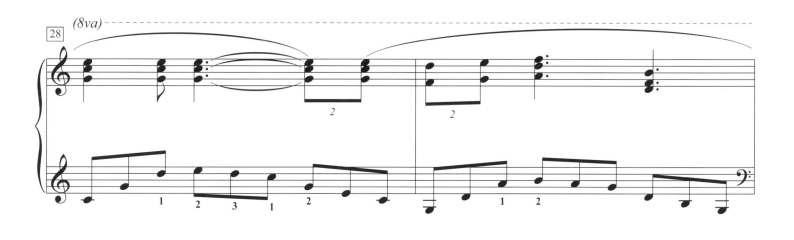

Ukrainian Bell Carol

By Mykola Leontovych
Arranged by Jennifer Linn

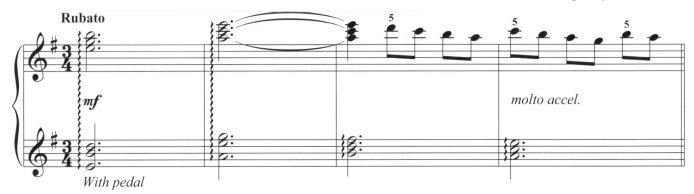

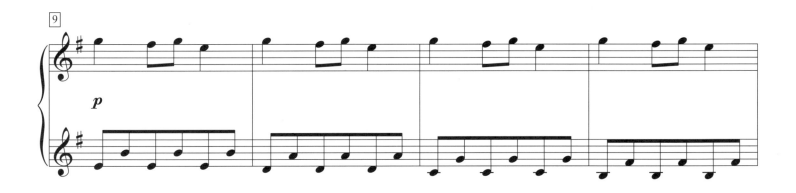

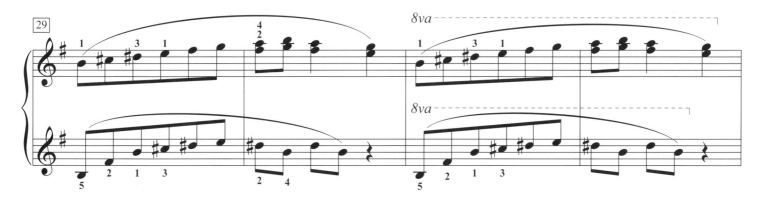

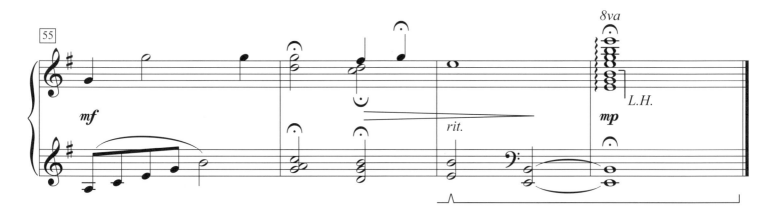

Gesù Bambino
(The Infant Jesus)

Traditional Italian
Arranged by Jennifer Linn

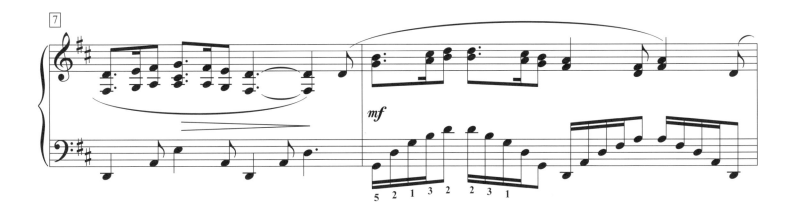

28

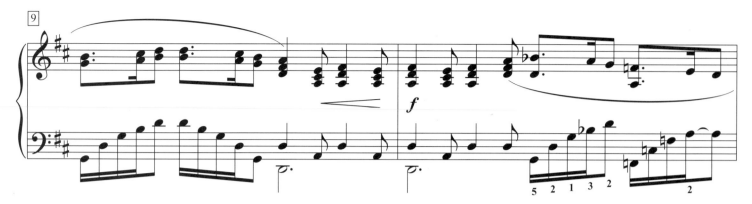

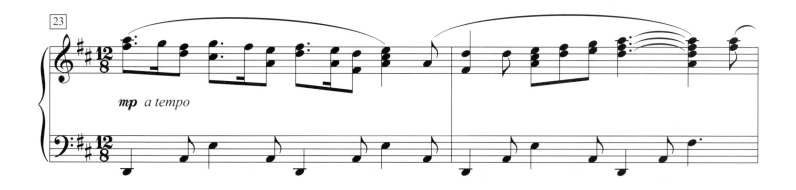

Cantique de Noël
(O Holy Night)

By Adolphe Adam
Arranged by Jennifer Linn

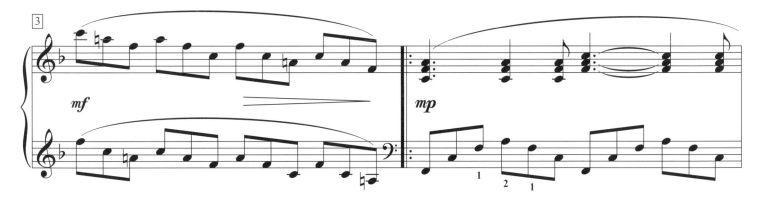

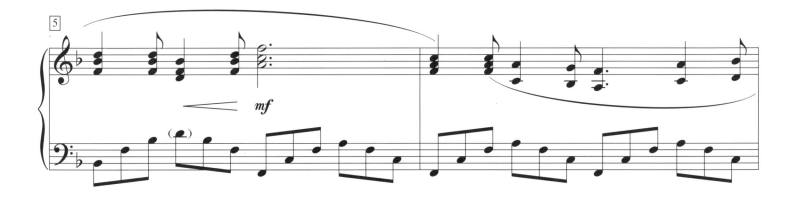

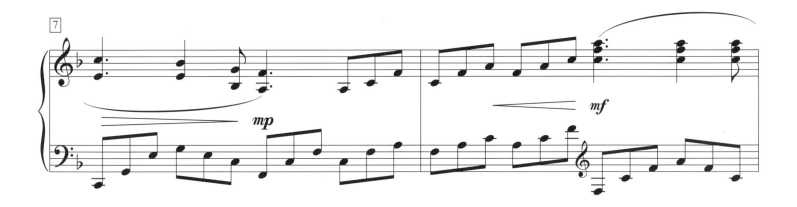

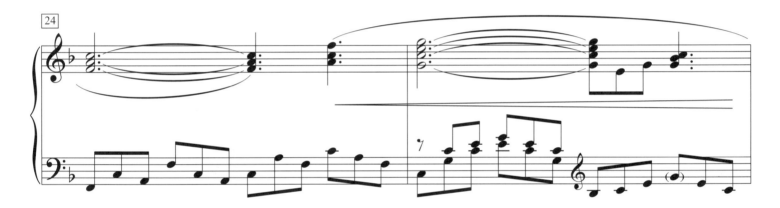